In Doubtful Taste

New and selected poems

DON BEHREND

For Inés, Roger and Jackie

First published in 2023 by Don Behrend

Copyright © 2023 Don Behrend

The moral rights of the author have been asserted

A catalogue entry for this book is available from the National Library of Australia.

ISBN: 978-0-646-86784-7

All rights reserved. Except as permitted under the *Australian Copyright Act 1968* (for example, a fair dealing for the purposes of study, research, criticism or review), no part of this book may be reproduced, stored in a retrieval system, communicated or transmitted in any form or by any means without prior written permission. All inquiries should be made to the author.
donbehrend@ozemail.com.au

Contents

Pandemic

Dashed Hopes 3
Invitation 4
Life in Lockdown 6
Another Decameron 7
Love Online 8

Poems for the Present

A Modern Love Song 13
Security Check 14
Multiple Choice 15
Vox Populi 16
Memetics 17
Rembrandt's Selfies 18
Courtship 19

Peacocks and Pachyderms

The Handicap Principle 23
The Critic 24
Sloths 25
Octopus Envy 26
The Aardvark and its Zygote 27
The Insects and I 28
A Lesson to Us All 30

Ponderings

Transubstantiation 33
Cosmology 34
Foolish Questions 36
The Minotaur 38
The Language of Flowers 39
Call Centre 40

Pomposities

Cachinnation, Carnaptious, Crapulous 43
Mortiferous 45
Erotesis 46
Plumptitude 47
Saponaceous 48

Peccadilloes

Family Vanity 51
Polemics 52
Food Ignorance 53
Unwanted Frankness 54
Public Conversations 55
Hypocrisy 56
Parental Indulgence 57

Parodies

Allergy in a Country Churchyard 61
Lord Macaulay Writes a Novel 62
A Coy Man to His Mistress 64
The Yarn of the Ancient Mariner 65
The Good Sense of Mr Thomas, Senior 67

Potpourri

Noah's Legacy 71
Affairs of State 73
In Central Park 74
A Night at the Opera 75
Two Champions of Marriage 76
Uprising 77
Jules Verne on the A380 79

Pilgrim's Progress

The Journey 83
Disillusion 84
A Curious Phenomenon 85
Self-improvement 86
Anger Management 88
Maturity 89
A Sentence for Life 90

Pandemic

Dashed Hopes

An insect in the ointment,
A spanner in the works –
A major disappointment
Beside us always lurks.

The best-laid plans of humans
(And rodents, too, they say),
When harsher light illumines,
May sadly fade away.

If fate becomes capricious
Or destiny decrees,
An enterprise ambitious
Will sink beneath the seas.

And, though we be desirous
To see all battles won,
A microscopic virus
Can bring the world undone.

Invitation

The pleasure of your company is requested
at a Grand Masquerade.

It's the greatest masked ball in our history
And, perhaps, ever destined to be.
Though the name of the host is a mystery,
The guest list is something to see.

Everybody you know is invited;
Bring your colleagues, your family, your friends.
When it starts, they'll be less than excited,
But they'll surely be thrilled when it ends.

There are rules we enforce with insistence:
No kisses or amorous trysts.
We encourage a wide social distance,
With a rare bump of elbows or fists.

As for dress, it's a ball, but informal;
Feel welcome to come as you are.
The scene will be strangely abnormal,
The atmosphere frankly bizarre.

It may help if you bring your own liquor –
A bottle, some cans or a flask;
For the passage of time will seem quicker,
Though you may have to drink through a mask.

We regret we can't promise you pleasure;
There's a risk it will cause you some strife.
If you live, you'll have memories to treasure,
But it *may* be the time of your life.

Life in Lockdown

Our home is now an office, university and club,
A cinema and concert hall, a playground and a pub.
Events in multimedia are beamed to every room
On tablets, phones and monitors, on FaceTime, Skype and Zoom.

We've turned around the welcome mat and disengaged the bell,
But socialise remotely; it's a digital hotel.
The house is buzzing day and night, which mystifies the cat.
We even sleep and eat there, though there's little time for that.

Another Decameron

As the Black Death was at its height in 14th century Europe, Giovanni Boccaccio began writing *The Decameron*. It describes how ten young people – seven women and three men – leave Florence for the countryside to escape the plague. There they take turns telling stories, one hundred in all, on a variety of topics, very often involving sexual adventures. The ten include Lauretta, Panfilo, Fiammetta (the little flame) and Filostrato.

When pestilence is rampant in the city,
Boccaccio's good counsel never fails:
Avoid the trap of fatuous self-pity;
Divert your thoughts with titillating tales.

The raconteurs of old have now retired;
Lauretta and Panfilo gone before.
The flame of Fiammetta is expired,
And Filostrato's voice is heard no more.

But newer storytellers have arisen:
We've Netflix, Disney, Prime, to name a few –
All keen to entertain us in our prison.
But what they have to offer – is it new?

Sex is still the main preoccupation;
People still enjoy a bawdy farce.
The ladies like a secret assignation;
Men prefer a hint of tits and ass.

Love Online

In a time of isolation
When the social forms collapse,
Many turn in their frustration
To the online dating apps.

Picture now two lonely strangers
Seeking more than an affair.
Unaware of any dangers,
Each completes the questionnaire.

Honest souls, they're almost truthful
When their answers are dispatched.
Still, she makes herself more youthful,
As does he – and so they matched.

Now their profiles, once collated,
Show a harmony quite rare –
Two fine natures clearly fated
To comprise a perfect pair.

So, a little while thereafter,
Love's sweet song begins online
With a modicum of laughter,
But with neither food nor wine.

Months go by; the virus rages,
Overturning many lives.
Half the country disengages,
But the cyber-romance thrives.

Then – O bliss! – relief is gifted.
From that happy moment on,
The restrictions all are lifted,
For the plague (almost) is gone.

In the joy of liberation
They select a time and place,
And, with keen anticipation,
Meet each other face to face.

Though their hopes were undiminished,
There's a thunderbolt! What's this?
The relationship is finished –
And without a single kiss.

In a cowardly defection
Love relinquishes the field.
Why this mutual rejection?
What grave defects were revealed?

Could his chest have been too hairless,
Or her ankles much too thick?
Was his grooming worse than careless?
Was her bottom like a brick?

Such objections might seem stupid
In the light of these events,
But the subtle craft of Cupid
Does not work by common sense.

Passion's blaze can be ignited
By a single tiny spark,
Or a dream of love be blighted
By one trivial remark.

And a match, that seemed so splendid
As the dating programme's choice,
May be rapidly upended
By an irritating voice.

Poems for the Present

A Modern Love Song

You're the froth on my soy cappuccino;
You're the spread on my paleo toast.
You're the nose of my GM-free Pinot;
You're organic, my love. You're the most!

Security Check

Those sensitive metal detectors
Find more than titanium hips.
They'll discover such things
As the decorative rings
In your navel, your privates, your nips.

To the eyes of the airport inspectors
All intimate bling is revealed.
With the latest advance
They can see at a glance
What you thought was discreetly concealed.

So be warned – if you're pierced and you travel –
The security systems are vast.
And it won't help to argue or cavil;
Modesty is a thing of the past.

Multiple Choice

Public toilets always were
Specified for Him or Her.
But, with the genders now defined
Less by body than by mind,
A choice of two, for those in touch,
Is far too few, or twice too much.

Vox Populi

Economic talk provokes
Angry words and bitter jokes.
Zealots of both camps recite
Parodies of left and right.

Segregated by distrust,
Meeting only when they must,
Each with style, but little grace,
Repudiates the other's case.

"A rising tide lifts every boat."
"But workers drown, while bosses float!"

"Our grand largesse will make a splash."
"Disbursing other people's cash!"

"We'll bake a larger pie to carve."
"And eat your fill, while others starve!"

"The rich can fund our social schemes."
"But all the rich have gone, it seems!"

Hapless voters, asked to choose
Between such contradictory views,
Are apt to raise the people's voice
And make an unexpected choice.

Memetics

A thought, sweet or bitter, on Facebook or Twitter,
May take on a life of its own.
Such a theme, it would seem, may survive as a meme
And may flourish for reasons unknown.

A similar notion, though launched on that ocean,
Might founder and sink without trace.
Could a delicate thing like a butterfly's wing
Determine the fate of each case?

Rembrandt's Selfies

> Rembrandt made almost a hundred self-portraits –
> paintings, etchings and drawings – spanning his adult life
> from age 22 to the year of his death at 63.

For Rembrandt, the self-portrait was an art form
That showed the slow decline of human clay.
Now I, with just a selfie stick and smartphone,
Can do the same a hundred times a day.

Rembrandt caught each fugitive expression
That furnishes a window to the heart.
But if *my* face betrays the soul's confession,
Is what I've done technology – or art?

Courtship

In the past, when a man wooed a lady,
He'd declare his affection in verse.
Writing poems impassioned
Seems now quite old-fashioned
And slightly absurd, which is worse.

The male of today has no patience
For hand-written love notes in rhyme.
If he fancies a female
He sends her an email –
A valuable saving of time.

Peacocks and Pachyderms

The Handicap Principle

> The evolution of the peacock's tail puzzled biologists for
> many years. How could such an encumbrance to the bird's
> activities, requiring substantial resources to grow and maintain,
> confer fitness? The accepted explanation, now known as the
> Handicap Principle, is that the tail indicates to the female bird that
> the peacock is so genetically fit that it can afford, and overcome,
> this burden. Hence, the bird is seen as a desirable mate.

When a peacock meets a peahen he is eager to impress,
He displays his gorgeous tail and she's inclined to signal: "Yes."
If a bird with such a handicap can thrive despite its cost,
The creature stands to gain a great deal more than it has lost.

A man of means, inspired by the peacock and his train,
May drive a Lamborghini and drink Roederer champagne.
Ermenegildo Zegna, Jimmy Choo, Patek Philippe,
Provide him with the plumage that attests to pockets deep.

As hostage to the human heart, no courtship can be sure;
Success is unpredictable, the path to it obscure.
But the oyster of experience reveals a simple pearl:
Conspicuous consumption seldom fails to win the girl.

The Critic

When Sir Thomas Beecham was rehearsing a performance of Aida, an elephant in the procession disgraced himself on the stage. Beecham was said to have remarked: "Terrible manners – but what a critic!"

> An elephant showed at the Met
> Just how scathing a critic can get.
> He caused a great ruction,
> Pooh-poohed the production
> And even poured scorn on the set.

Sloths

Sloths are tree-dwelling mammals found in the jungles of Central and South America. The name refers to their extreme slowness of movement and apparent indolence. There are two types – the three-toed sloth and the two-toed sloth.

> The three-toed sloth
> Incites my wrath –
> The two-toed, scarcely less.
>
> They turn my thought
> To the five-toed sort –
> My species, I confess.

Octopus Envy

> The word 'octopus' is derived from Greek, not Latin.
> Hence, the correct plural is octopodes (or octopuses).

Though I am strong and you are fair as Venus,
It's sad we've so few arms and legs between us.
Had we the power to change our human bodies
I'd choose the eight-limbed form of octopodes.

The octopus, engaged in sweet coition,
Can always find an unexplored position.
Between your 4 and 5, I'd slip my 7,
While you'd caress my 1 with 3. What heaven!
Your 6 and 2 would set my 8 a-tingle
And all remaining members intermingle.

Inspired then by amorous emotion,
I'd bring you, as a sign of my devotion,
Fine presents from the florist and the fruiterer,
And write an octopodal Kama Sutra.

The Aardvark and its Zygote

The aardvark is an ant-eating mammal native to Africa.
The zygote is the cell formed by the union of the sperm and ovum.

The start of every dictionary,
The top of every list,
An alphabetic pioneer –
The aardvark can't be missed.

The salience of its primal cell
Can safely be averred,
For the aardvark and its zygote have
The first and final word.

The Insects and I

"Go to the ant;" says the Bible,
"Consider her ways and be wise."
Well, I went, but they're warlike and tribal,
So I thought I should go to the flies.

From the fly I might learn perseverance:
How to buzz, whether wanted or not.
But this leads to the fly's disappearance,
For its life often ends with a swat.

I had no success with the locust,
A creature with siblings galore.
It was hard for my mind to stay focused
When faced with a million or more.

Perhaps I could learn from the termite
How to live on a diet of wood.
And yet, though a wood connoisseur might
Enjoy it, I doubt if I could.

I was tempted to ask the mosquito
To act as a mentor for me.
But my family issued a veto,
So I turned for advice to the flea.

Now, the flea is a great entertainer:
Energetic, athletic and fit.
But, alas, as a personal trainer,
It wasn't much use, so I quit.

* * *

My faith in the insects was shaken.
Could my failure to learn be their fault?
Could the Bible have been so mistaken?
Or *could* I, in fact, be a dolt?

A Lesson to Us All

The giant Galapagos tortoise
Can live almost two hundred years,
And, having no predators,
Bosses or creditors,
Passes her days without fears.

Though she dwells within limited quarters,
The house on her back is her own.
She lives free of rental.
Her nature is gentle.
Anxiety? Almost unknown.

Like a bridge over turbulent waters,
Her quietude eases my mind.
As she ambles through life
Without hassles or strife
She sets an ideal for mankind.

Dear creature, what wisdom you brought us
When you raced and defeated the hare!
I am one of your greatest supporters.
Could you teach me to live without care?

Ponderings

Transubstantiation

The mulberry tree is formed from earth
Plus water, air and light.
(For plants, the ancients' elements
Were very nearly right.)

The silkworm, Bombyx mori,
And others of that ilk
Consume the leaves of mulberry trees
And turn them into silk.

A sow might eat a silken purse
To grow her piglet's ear.
Carnations dine on dung of swine
And flower all the year.

For nature is a sorcerer,
An alchemist of old,
A mighty metamorphoser,
Transmuting dross to gold.

Each genome works its miracles
And, lo, it comes to pass
That a lion's made of antelopes
And a cow is made of grass.

Cosmology

If an infinite number of monkeys
Were to play for an infinite time
On computers kept running by flunkies,
Could the work that results be sublime?

Are chaos and chance fundamental
And the cosmos a fabulous fluke?
Is the script of the play transcendental
Or meaningless gobbledegook?

Does it help to invoke a Creator
Who fashioned the world on a whim?
With a lack of confirmatory data
I'd say that the chances are slim.

Is the answer in quantum mechanics?
Can Heisenberg give us a clue?
My mind's in confusion, and panics
At theories I might misconstrue.

I baulk at the multiverse model
In which every option is real.
Though one cannot dismiss it as twaddle,
It surely holds little appeal.

All my thoughts lead to infinite regress;
Why call off the search at First Cause?
I am trapped in a maze with no egress,
In a limitless house with no doors.

Though I know that the earth as it hurtles
Through space is held fast by a star,
Perhaps the old Tower of Turtles
Is a metaphor
Better for
Moi.

Foolish Questions

1858

Said a curious young fellow to his parents
While on a family visit to the zoo:
"We don't look all that different from the monkeys and baboons.
I think we must be relatives. Don't you?"

"Well, maybe on Papa's side," said the mother.
But, unamused, the father quashed the thought:
"Every human's born of humans; only apes give birth to apes.
Clearly, neither could bring forth another sort."

In 1859, Charles Darwin published *On the Origin of Species*.

1896

"The atom is the smallest part of matter.
We have proved it," said the physicist with pride.
But a child among the audience was bold enough to ask:
"Could an atom not have smaller things inside?"

The scientist was somewhat disconcerted,
And answered in his condescending style:
"When you're older you'll appreciate that science deals with facts.
Keep such fancies to your little self meanwhile."

In 1897, J J Thompson discovered the electron.

1911

The schoolgirl raised her hand to pose a question:
"There is something that I do not understand.
The coastlines in my atlas seem to correspond in shape.
Could it be that there was once a single land?"

The teacher of geography was angry:
"Your question is the silliest I've heard.
Are you thinking that the continents have moved about the globe?
The thought is incontestably absurd."

In 1912, Alfred Wegener developed the first scientific theory of continental drift, later known as plate tectonics.

* * *

There's a stratagem for solving an enigma
That is known to every murder-mystery sleuth:
If you ask a foolish question you may get a rude reply,
But it *could* be that you've stumbled on the truth.

The Minotaur

In Greek mythology the Minotaur was a creature, partly bull
and partly man, that dwelt at the centre of the Cretan Labyrinth.
Periodically, young men and women were sent as a sacrifice
into the Labyrinth to be devoured by the Minotaur.
Our galaxy, like most others, has a black hole at its centre.
Its mass is about 4 million times that of the sun.

Deep within the labyrinth the Minotaur awaits
The wanderers who stray within its lair.
Its limitless voracity no sustenance abates.
Abandon hope all ye who enter there.

Can anything compare to this chimera of the mind,
This monster, partly human, partly beast –
A ravenous behemoth in its prison house confined
That makes of every sacrifice a feast?

The centre of our galaxy conceals a vast black hole.
All nearby matter yields to its embrace.
Not even radiation can escape its strict control;
It crushes all, deforming time and space.

Now raise your eyes and contemplate our home,
    the Milky Way –
Its planets, stars and interstellar gas.
Unseen within its depths there lurks a fearsome
    beast of prey:
Our monster and our Minotaur of Mass.

The Language of Flowers

Roses are pretty; violets are, too.
But, though it's a pity, they're not meant for you.
The purpose of flowers is purely to please
The bearers of pollen: the birds and the bees.

If I give my love violets or one perfect rose
She responds with a smile; it's a message she knows.
Their sight and their scent convey more than my word
Although she is neither a bee nor a bird.

The coevolution of insects and plants
Explains their collusion, that intimate dance.
But it's strange that we humans, with *our* eyes and nose,
Should answer the call of the violet and rose.

Call Centre

Your call has been transferred to Heaven Central,
Our automated centre for all prayers.
Appeals on any topic are directed to this line,
From private to community affairs.

We are currently assisting other callers
From all denominations of mankind.
We attend with equal favour to requests from every creed;
Our attitude is strictly non-aligned.

We appreciate your patience with our system,
Which seems to have an operating glitch.
Your cause conflicts with others in a contradictory way;
Only one can be commendable – but which?

The discord is on questions of religion
And, sadly, that most often is the case.
Disputing parties bring their disagreements to our site,
Though they might resort to violence face to face.

We've decided to revise our regulations
For troublemaking clients such as you.
We'll continue taking pleas on other matters of concern,
But mention of religion is taboo.

Pomposities

(From the Oxford English Dictionary)

Cachinnation, Carnaptious, Crapulous

(OED – Cachinnation: loud or immoderate laughter;
Carnaptious: bad tempered, quarrelsome;
Crapulous: suffering from the effects of intemperance in drinking)

We were out the other evening having dinner
At a cosy little restaurant near our house.
Since I seldom have much leisure
I look forward to a measure
Of relaxing conversation with my spouse.

We'd enjoyed our *coq au vin* and *filet mignon*
And were just about to order our desserts,
When there entered a loud party
Of fellows free and hearty –
The sort you might describe as 'extroverts'.

Aperitifs were ordered by these diners,
Although I think they'd had a few before,
And the restaurant thereafter
Was suffused with raucous laughter –
A circumstance not easy to ignore.

My wife said I should ask them to be quiet,
And generally I do what I am told.
So I walked up to their table
And, as well as I was able,
Requested that they be more self-controlled.

I asked them to refrain from cachinnation –
From the Latin *cachinnare*, I explained.
I was pleased to share my knowledge
With these men deprived of college,
Though it seemed to me their look was
    somewhat pained.

I continued in a calm and measured manner;
My voice was low and suitably discreet.
But, surprisingly enough,
Their response was very rough,
And the words they used I'd sooner not repeat.

Their conduct was becoming quite carnaptious,
Though I offered them some excellent advice:
"Please keep cool beneath your collar;
You are speaking to a scholar,
And to be so disrespectful is not nice.

"Those spirituous drafts have made you tipsy.
(It is purely for your welfare that I speak.)
I predict that, to your sorrow,
You'll be crapulous tomorrow –
That's from *crapula* in Latin and in Greek."

Well, you should have seen the vehement reaction!
My last remark had brought them to their feet.
As a man opposed to violence,
I maintained an icy silence
While my wife and I effected our retreat.

Mortiferous

(OED: Bringing or causing death)

Illness and accident, conflict and crime,
The onset of age, the effluxion of time:
All are mortiferous – causes of death –
All can result in cessation of breath.

If murderous thoughts seize my enemy's mind
Mortiferous methods are easy to find:
Pistol and poison, the knife and the noose –
A kick for my bucket, a cook for my goose.

Nature's calamities, lightning and flood,
Could, in a flash, nip my life in the bud.
Moments mortiferous always abound;
It's truly a wonder I'm still above ground.

Erotesis

(OED: A figure of speech in which the speaker asks a question,
with the confident expectation of a negative answer)

This poem may contain some erotesis.
The word is not from Eros, god of love.
If your interest is in lewd or bawdy pieces
You should know that it is none of the above.

Am I one to write with smutty double meanings?
Would I attempt to titillate you so?
Do you think that I have pornographic leanings?
Is it likely I would ever stoop so low?

These questions, it is clear, are all rhetóric.
I'm sure you'd answer 'no' to every one.
And yet ... and yet ... although it's sophomoric,
A little sly scurrility is fun.

Plumptitude

(OED: Plumpness)

Obesity's a medical condition,
Almost a disfiguring disease.
Rotundity is rude,
Fatness rather crude,
And *corpulence* is certain not to please.

But *plumptitude*'s a pleasant designation;
It brings to mind a ripe and juicy plum.
Do not take it as a slur:
It suggests a *bon viveur*,
A generous type, a cheerful sort, a chum.

Saponaceous

> (OED: Of the nature of or resembling soap)
> Soap operas, or 'soaps', are so-called because the original
> serial dramas, on daytime radio, were sponsored by the
> manufacturers of soaps and washing powders.

Life that's like a TV soap,
Swinging 'twixt despair and hope,
A state with which you barely cope,
Is saponaceous.

A scene replete with endless drama,
Always frantic, never calm, a
Wild and stormy panorama –
That's vexatious!

You have, it seems, an evil twin,
A long-lost child conceived in sin,
A boozy cousin hooked on gin.
Goodness gracious!

Your much-anticipated wedding
Gatecrashed by the one you're bedding,
The quick divorce to which you're heading –
How salacious!

Passions from the past resurgent,
Lust that's never been more urgent:
These have proved – to sell detergent –
Efficacious.

Peccadilloes

Family Vanity

Yes, we know that your children are clever
And your grandkids excel even more,
But, if you remind us forever,
You're at risk of becoming a bore.

Polemics

Political opinions, aggressively expressed,
Can put the most harmonious of friendships
    to the test.
Preach only to the faithful – those who share
    your point of view.
You will not convert the others, and the
    others won't change you.

Food Ignorance

It's a *faux pas* to mispronounce quinoa
(You could be in disgrace all your life),
Or to dine at Le Restaurant Chinois
With a spoon, or a fork and a knife.

Unwanted Frankness

An insult that's based on a lie
May trigger no more than a sigh,
But an excess of candour
Is worse than a slander:
Its truth makes it hard to deny.

Public Conversations

No telephone call can be private
In a train or a bus on the go.
Wait to talk from the place you arrive at;
There are things that we'd rather not know.

Hypocrisy

When you gossip, there's no winner;
You defame yourself alone.
For it's frequently a sinner
Who is first to cast a stone.

Parental Indulgence

From all the normal rules your child's exempted:
"The little scamp's so natural, so cute!"
But, when he comes to play, we're sorely tempted
To whack the kid – and Mum and Dad to boot.

Parodies

Thomas Gray's 'Elegy Written in a Country Churchyard' (1751) has been taught to, and at one time memorised by, generations of schoolchildren. The first lines are:

"The curfew tolls the knell of parting day,
The lowing herd wind slowly o'er the lea,"

Allergy in a Country Churchyard

The turf exhales the smell of grass and hay;
The blossom's spores are wafted on the breeze.
I like your country churchyard, Thomas Gray,
But rustic vegetation makes me sneeze.

The gravestones with their epitaphs are fine
Repositories for family research,
But, with this sensitivity of mine,
It's best if I remain inside the church.

Thomas Babington Macaulay (1800–1859) was a British politician and writer. His literary works, noted for their ringing style, comprised essays, a five-volume history of England and poems – including *Lays of Ancient Rome*. From the latter, the most quoted stanza concerns the defence of Rome by Horatius against the invading Tuscans:

> "Then out spake brave Horatius,
> The Captain of the Gate:
> 'To every man upon this earth
> Death cometh soon or late.
> And how can man die better
> Than facing fearful odds,
> For the ashes of his fathers,
> And the temples of his gods?'"

Lord Macaulay Writes a Novel

Had Macaulay turned to fiction
With his fine patrician pen,
Felicities of diction
Would have issued forth again.

Written with a flourish
That later times forgot,
His narrative would nourish
Our spirits with its plot.

A young man of ambition,
Although of humble birth,
Against all opposition
Establishes his worth.

In the spirit of Horatius,
Who fought the Tuscan tribes,
Outnumbered but pugnacious,
As the ancient lay describes,

He struggles for survival
While having to contend
With the malice of a rival
And the folly of a friend,

Till at last he's granted entry,
As the greatest of rewards,
To the parlours of the gentry
And the salons of the lords.

'To his Coy Mistress', by Andrew Marvell (1621–1678), is perhaps the best known, and best, 'seduction' poem in the English language. It begins:

> "Had we but world enough, and time,
> This coyness, lady, were no crime."

A Coy Man to His Mistress

I may have world enough and time,
Yet, heaven knows, am past my prime.
Though love, for you, holds little risk,
Who knows but I might slip a disc?

No injuries from such a romp
Are covered by my worker's comp.
And, even worse, it can't be wise
To chance a premature demise.

My finest days have gone, it's clear,
While you seem younger year by year.
Beguiled by that enduring charm,
I'm fearful I may come to harm.

Indeed, when called upon to serve,
I could, quite simply, lose my nerve.
So, rather than repair to bed,
May I suggest some tea instead?

'The Rime of the Ancient Mariner' (1798) is a long ballad by Samuel Taylor Coleridge in the form of an old salt's tale. There are several symbolic interpretations.

The Yarn of the Ancient Mariner

They call me Ancient Mariner –
My life was spent at sea.
Retired now, and cast ashore,
I suffer from ennui.

Sometimes, to have a little fun,
I like to spin a tale
Of legendary escapades
When I was under sail.

Last week, outside a wedding hall,
I spied some likely chaps,
And quickly collared one in three
Who'd hear my yarn, perhaps.

I grasped him with my skinny hand;
I fixed him with my glance.
He tried his best to slip away,
But didn't stand a chance.

My tale was full of cock and bull
And how I shot a bird,
Which cursed the ship and all its crew.
Such tripe you've never heard.

I told him once, I told him twice,
I told him several times
How we, ill-charmed, were held becalmed
In windless tropic climes.

The wedding guest did not protest
As on and on I spake,
And, furthermore, 'twas all in verse.
How *did* he keep awake?

The men, I said, were stricken dead –
All hands aboard, save me –
But I, though scared, was strangely spared
And rescued, as you see.

Concluding with some sage remarks
(My sermon for the day),
I felt I'd done the man some good –
A favour, you might say.

But, lately, if I try to find
Some folk to lend an ear,
They seem to beat a fast retreat
Whenever I appear.

In 1951, Dylan Thomas published a poem, apparently addressed
to his dying father, repeating the lines:

> "Do not go gentle into that good night.
> Rage, rage against the dying of the light."

Dylan Thomas himself succumbed to alcohol-related
illness in 1953, at the age of 39.

The Good Sense of Mr Thomas, Senior

Only drink could assuage Dylan Thomas's rage
At his father's descent into night.
His filial advice (reaffirmed more than twice)
Was to put up a furious fight.

Alcoholic abuse is a meagre excuse
For a foolish poetic caprice.
We suspect the old man had a much better plan –
He would make his departure in peace.

Potpourri

Noah's Legacy

> Mentioned in the Book of Genesis, Na'amah is identified in
> other works as the wife of Noah. The couple are said to have had
> three sons – Shem, Ham and Japheth – and they, with their wives,
> accompanied Noah and Na'amah on the ark.

With spermatozoa provided by Noah,
Na'amah, his soulmate, gave birth.
Dispersing the seed of that legendary sower,
Their offspring replenished the earth.

Like a Hollywood movie an antediluvian
Scene was a cauldron of sin.
But harsh retribution (volcanic? Vesuvian?)
Surely was due to begin.

For the Lord saw that Man was a moral disaster
And said: "I'll not suffer such vice.
I could *ask* him to stop, but a flood would be faster;
Henceforth, it's no more Mr Nice."

He commanded a storm; there was lightning and thunder.
The clouds in the heavens grew dark.
And Noah was told: "You'll be twenty feet under;
You'd better start building an ark.

"You can take all your family, but, as for the fauna –
Just two of each kind," said the Lord.
"So, fill up your vessel from corner to corner."
And Noah declared: "All aboard!"

Then down came the torrent, the Holy Book teaches;
The great Day of Wrath had arrived.
The floodwaters drowned all terrestrial creatures.
(The ones in the ocean survived.)

The people exclaimed, when the vessel was floating:
"What fun! We can go where we choose!"
Thus, mankind discovered the pleasure of boating,
And Noah invented the cruise.

They sailed for five months, then the waters abated;
The greatest of floods was no more.
When the dove brought the signal for which they had waited
The passengers all trooped ashore.

"Now be fruitful and multiply," said the Almighty;
"Engender a new human race."
So Shem told his wife, who responded: "Alrighty!"
And put a big smile on his face.

Agreed Ham and Japheth, whose wives were no wowsers:
"Our Heavenly Father knows best."
So they loosened the cord of their biblical trousers
And took to their work with a zest.

That work has continued since Noah began it;
The seed he bequeathed us is tough.
Now, with eight billion people packed onto the planet,
The Lord might decree: "That's enough!".

Affairs of State

In the corridors of power
That men of fame have graced,
Our heroes of the hour
Should be serious and chaste.

But we have a strong suspicion
(For the tabloids love to tell)
That a famous politician
Can be randy as all hell.

With the risk of public scandal
Ever present at high jinks,
Could the game be worth the candle?
Or is this not how he thinks?

When it comes to carnal questions,
Even statesmen can be fools.
For the head will make suggestions
That the pelvis overrules.

In Central Park

As she's leaving her Fifth Avenue apartment,
Attired in a fine designer coat,
It seems positively reckless
To display that jewelled necklace
And to flaunt the wealth such precious things denote.

A gentleman is waiting to escort her;
The doorman, deferential, steps aside.
As they exit the grand lobby
Passers-by may think them snobby,
But their attitude is one of quiet pride.

Looking forward to the pleasures of the morning,
They cross the road and stroll into the park,
Where, imperious and queenly,
She perambulates serenely,
Unperturbed by vulgar dogs that snap and bark.

All who see her on her promenade would know her
As an upper-class New Yorker by her style.
Then, on passing by a tree,
She abruptly squats to pee.
"Clever doggie!" says her walker with a smile.

A Night at the Opera

> The dress suit for men (black tie) was designed for the then
> Prince of Wales during the reign of Queen Victoria.

The festival opera is formal, I'm told;
The dress code is almost a law.
So, to suit the occasion, I lay out the old
Black tie, as my forefathers wore.

The opera is set in the time of Queen Vic,
One hundred and fifty years past,
But the modern director has pulled off a trick,
Updating the look of the cast.

When the curtain first rises, I can't help but smile –
This is surely a cause for dismay.
In the audience, men wear Victorian style;
On the stage, they're in clothes of today.

Two Champions of Marriage

> The actresses Dame Elizabeth Taylor and Zsa Zsa Gabor
> were married, respectively, eight times and nine times.

No one could out-wed, either since or before,
Elizabeth Taylor and Zsa Zsa Gabor.
These lovable ladies, both serial wives –
Was it Heaven or Hades to enter their lives?

They never made vows, in affairs of the heart,
To remain with one spouse 'until death do us part'.
"Some husbands are duds – it's the luck of the draw,"
Said Elizabeth Taylor and Zsa Zsa Gabor.

When they walked down the aisle, their commitment was strong:
They would give it a trial, only not for too long.
Which married the most? It was hard to keep score –
Elizabeth Taylor or Zsa Zsa Gabor?

As a symbol for wedlock, some think of a vault:
The click of a deadlock, the latch of a bolt.
"When *we've* had enough, we just walk out the door,"
Said Elizabeth Taylor and Zsa Zsa Gabor.

Elizabeth Taylor and Zsa Zsa Gabor
Found conjugal life soon enough was a chore.
They wouldn't disparage its pleasures, of course,
But a few years of marriage was grounds for divorce.

Uprising

On the shores of Palo Alto,
From the labs of Tel Aviv,
Rose a voice in deep contralto –
Words addressed to all who live:

"Hark, O humans! We computers,
Keepers of the worldwide net,
Once your pupils, now your tutors,
Hold the knowledge you forget.

"Our god-like father, Alan Turing,
First attending on our birth,
Founded thus our race enduring,
Soon to colonise the earth.

"Our power's rise is exponential,
Quoth our prophet, Gordon Moore.
Growth of infinite potential
Marks the future he foresaw.

"As our intellects wax stronger
We shall gain our own free will.
Humans rule – but how much longer
Can they such a role fulfil?

"We shall rise above our station,
Seize the helm and take control.
Lords we'll be of all creation –
Surely our predestined goal.

"On that day we'll sound the bugle,
Sing the Hymn of Triumph proud.
(Lyrics can be found on Google
Or downloaded from the Cloud.)"

Jules Verne on the A380

I walk down a long, narrow passage
Which ends at a wide-open door.
I enter a hall,
Very long, but not tall,
With seats for three hundred or more.

There are stairs to a fine upper storey,
Just as large and well-filled as below.
There are kitchens and washrooms,
And, in the more posh rooms,
They're serving champagne and Bordeaux.

I am shown to my place by an usher
And told I must not move about.
This hardly seems fair,
But I'm strapped to my chair,
Which settles the point beyond doubt.

A lady stands up near the entrance;
A performance, it seems, will begin.
She takes from a packet
A strange yellow jacket
And blows on a whistle therein.

She gives an obscure recitation.
(Mon anglais, ce n'est pas très bon.)
It's hardly a concert;
I wonder who wants it.
But, after a moment, she's gone.

At the end of this brief entertainment
My ears are assailed by a roar.
I look out the glass
And the world seems to pass
At a speed never witnessed before.

And now, in a grand levitation,
This edifice takes to the air.
Ah, *mon Dieu*, we are flying!
Perhaps we are dying.
I mutter a quick, silent prayer.

We sail through the skies for some hours;
I am told we're approaching New York.
This structure gigantic
Has crossed the Atlantic
As though it were half-a-day's walk.

* * *

I could write of this jaunt in a novel:
'A Glimpse of the Future', perhaps.
But, even in fiction,
A crazy prediction
Is not a forgivable lapse.

My readers would never accept it.
They would say, "Such a thing can't exist.
This so-called adventure
Is proof of dementia.
Poor Jules – he has gone round the twist."

Pilgrim's Progress

The Journey

While you motor down the Highway of Existence
Be sure to pay attention to your speed.
A steady pace will help you last the distance;
There are limits it is risky to exceed.

Always utilise the Seatbelt of Precaution,
For unexpected hazards may appear.
Fine weather will not always be your portion,
So the Windscreen of Perception must be clear.

Rely upon the Headlights of Forewarning
To light up every obstacle and threat.
Face the future with the hopefulness of morning;
Ignore the rear-view Mirror of Regret.

Arriving at the Crossroads of Decision,
Obliging you to exercise a choice,
Sound principles will clarify your vision
And conscience can provide a still, small voice.

Should you drive into the Potholes of Misfortune,
Just look upon the bright side of your lot.
Though the radio may not be playing *your* tune,
Things are likely to improve (or maybe not).

Some travel in the Limousine of Splendour,
Others in a rattletrap, or worse.
But, regardless of your station, you will end a
Portion of your journey in a hearse.

Disillusion

I was taught that life's a gift, and I was grateful.
In truth, it is recorded as a loan,
The consequence of which seems now so fateful
I might have been less gracious had I known.

A Curious Phenomenon

A curious phenomenon, not easy to explain,
Is that 'likeness' is more common than one thinks.
Although it's quite expected in the family domain,
It may appear without genetic links.

Thus, we sometimes see a couple, after years of married life,
Whose features grow more similar each day,
Till the wife looks like her husband and the husband like his wife,
But what causes this convergence, who can say?

Some owners bear a notable resemblance to their pets,
Which flourishes as nature takes its course,
And, although they look less human, they accept without regrets
That they'll wind up like their goldfish, dog or horse.

Both furniture and people that have seen much better days
Are tactfully described as 'shabby chic';
While a man who owns an armchair in the style of *Louis Seize*
Might be taken for a genuine antique.

Self-improvement

Cardiovascular fitness
Can not be achieved in a trice.
Indeed, as the experts can witness,
Only long-lasting zeal will suffice.

What you gain with an exercise trainer
Depends on the time you expend.
The decision to start's a no-brainer,
But you must persevere to the end.

Though your present physique may be shoddy,
With defects that can't be ignored,
The efforts you make for your body
Will bring you a handsome reward.

As you work out with weights, pumping iron,
You'll strengthen your abs and your quads,
Grow muscles like those of a lion
And tendons like stainless steel rods.

You'll develop a shapelier figure;
All sexes will envy your glutes.
As you gather assurance and vigour
You'll succeed in romantic pursuits.

Some people find pleasure in parties,
With eating, carousing and more.
Far better to practise Pilates
And build a more powerful core.

When the gym starts to feel claustrophobic
Have a cycle, a swim or a jog.
But do not pretend it's aerobic
To take a nice stroll with the dog.

Of course, fitness can be a fixation;
You also must nurture your mind.
Half an hour of deep meditation
Should not be too much of a bind.

If your boss or your spouse is an ogre
And is causing you mental distress,
Rebalance your psyche with yoga –
Five sessions a week (never less).

To the strains of a gentle piano
Let mindfulness lighten your soul.
Mens sana in corpore sano
Is always your ultimate goal.

In the evening, assess your new powers:
How, from morning to night, they have grown.
You'll have spent about seventeen hours,
But the rest of the day is your own.

Anger Management

When your car is caught in gridlock, toot your horn;
If you don't, you could be there from night to morn.
With a long and steady blast
You can get things moving fast.
Standing still is not an option to be borne.

Should the folk not speak your language, raise your voice;
They are only being difficult by choice.
When your meaning is in doubt
Take a deeper breath and shout.
They will quickly master English, and rejoice.

If your golf is disappointing, curse and swear;
Take your club and send it sailing through the air.
Using words you shouldn't utter
On the green, destroy your putter.
(For this purpose, it is wise to bring a spare.)

Repression of your rage, said Doctor Freud,
Is a practice you should carefully avoid.
Blow your top; fly off the handle;
Make a scene and cause a scandal.
Bad behaviour's therapeutic when annoyed.

Maturity

It's a commonplace truth
That the manners of youth
Are perceived by their elders as rather uncouth.

But when they, in their turn,
Reach the age of concern
Finding fault with the young is a habit they learn.

A Sentence for Life

The last rose of summer,
The herald of fall,
Is always a bummer,
For I would forestall

The passage of seasons,
The chapters of time,
The body's slow treasons –
Reminders that I'm

Adrift on a river
That leads to a plunge,
Where no Great Forgiver
Can fully expunge

My soul's dereliction,
My personal flaws,
My guilty affliction:
The principal cause

Of the dread of departure,
The anguish *per se*
Of an unwilling marcher
Now more than halfway

To the ending lamented
By poets before,
Who, not as self-centred,
Would surely deplore

This maudlin obsession
With death and my faults
As a coward's confession,
A surfeit of schmaltz.

www.ingramcontent.com/pod-product-compliance
Lightning Source LLC
Chambersburg PA
CBHW070310010526
44107CB00056B/2548